CUTE CAT AND DOG PUZZLES

Kid Tested By
Eli AGE 6
& Jake AGE 9

HIGHLIGHTS PRESS
Honesdale, Pennsylvania

Welcome, Hidden Pictures Puzzlers!

When you finish a puzzle, check it off ☑. Good luck, and happy puzzling!

Contents

- *Purr*-fect Pup-cakes................ 4
- Playful *Purr*-maids 5
- Visiting the Vet 6–7
- Fluffy's Walk 8
- At the *Meow*-seum................. 9
- Kitty's Fish Tank 10
- Puppy Pilots 11
- Sweet Dreams 12–13
- A Game of Chase 14
- Family Road Trip 15
- Taco Cats and *Purr*-itos 16
- On the Trail........................ 17
- Dr. Katz's Time Machine.......... 18
- Cool Explorers..................... 19
- Pets in the Park................ 20–21
- Kitty Slurps........................ 22
- Bella's Favorite Stick.............. 23
- Cool Cats........................... 24
- Burying His Bone.................. 25
- Cozy Cuddlers..................... 26
- Pupp-eroni Pizzas................. 27
- Pet Wash 28–29
- Biking Buddies 30
- Itty-Bitty Puppies 31
- The Claw Salon................32–33
- The Longest Doggy.......... 34–35

- Which Dog Wins?................. 36
- Doggy's Bedtime.................. 37
- Lemonade, *Purr*-ity Please? 38
- Doggy's Trip to Space............ 39
- Cat Community 40–41
- Crafty Corgi-corns 42
- Pet Picture Palooza............... 43
- Cats in Boxes 44
- Nap Time.......................... 45
- Couch Pug-tato 46
- Kitty's Condo 47
- Cat Summer Camp 48
- Playground Pups.................. 49
- Underwater Pets 50–51
- Battle of Brains 52
- Animal Construction Crew....... 53
- Cat-erpillar's Forest.............. 54
- Puddle Jumpers................... 55
- Summer Vacation 56–57
- Making Biscuits................... 58
- Kitty Cat Club...................... 59
- *Meow*-ter Space................. 60
- Walking the Dogs................ 61
- Doggy Delivery.................... 62
- Dog Day at the Park 63
- Feline Fruits...................... 64–65

Cover Art by Gina Perry

- Furry Foods......................66
- Backpack Buddies................67
- Doggy Dash.......................68
- Sunken Treasure..................69
- Shipshape.....................70–71
- Best in Show.....................72
- Double Doggies...................73
- Park Romp.......................74
- Scaredy-Dog.....................75
- Fairy Friends..................76–77
- Bone Appètit..................78–79
- Lots of Stuffies..................80
- Backyard Bath....................81
- It's Bath Time!..................82
- Lab-racadabra....................83
- Granny Dogs..................84–85
- Kittens in Mittens................86
- Get a Good Sniff.................87
- Garage Band......................88
- So Much Yarn!....................89
- Beagle Bagels....................90
- Doggy's New Do..................91
- Look Who's Home!..........92–93
- Bulldog Meets Bullfrog..........94
- Cuddle Buddies..................95
- Tangled Up.......................96
- Bubbles, No Troubles............97
- A New Friend.................98–99
- Pugs and Kisses.................100
- Pups in Pajamas.................101
- Kit-teas.........................102
- Dog Volleyball..................103
- Howlin' Hound Dogs............104
- Poodles 'n' Noodles.............105
- The Coolest Cat Walk.....106–107
- Kitten Cuddles..................108
- Raining Cats and Dogs.........109
- Dogsled.........................110
- Apartment Kitty.................111
- A Cat Nap...................112–113
- Animal Swap.....................114
- Puppy Play Time................115
- Ain't Nothin' but a
  Hound Dog..................116–117
- Grand-dogs Calling..............118
- Dog Show........................119
- Doggy Dance-Off!..........120–121
- Robo Dogs.......................122
- Animal Zumba....................123
- Feline Fairy Tale................124
- Fluffy Cones....................125
- Window Kitties..................126
- Hide-and-Seek...................127
- Super Dogs......................128
- Game Night......................129
- Answer Keys................130–144

Purr-fect Pup-cakes

bell

crayon

slice of pizza

ladder

pennant

golf club

ring

cane

hot dog

toothbrush

bowl

ruler

bat

fish

envelope

comb

Playful *Purr*-maids

bowling pin

wedge of lemon

feather

doughnut

carrot

yo-yo

teacup

button

banana

Visiting the Vet

needle

feather

ticket

party hat

magnet

tooth

fork

flute

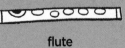
slice of bread

heart

popcorn

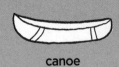
canoe

ice-cream cone

hockey stick

hammer

magnifying glass

banana

funnel

yo-yo

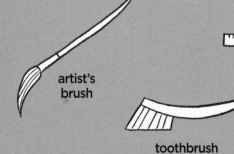
artist's brush

ruler

slice of pizza

toothbrush

waffle

envelope

7

Fluffy's Walk

At the Meow-seum

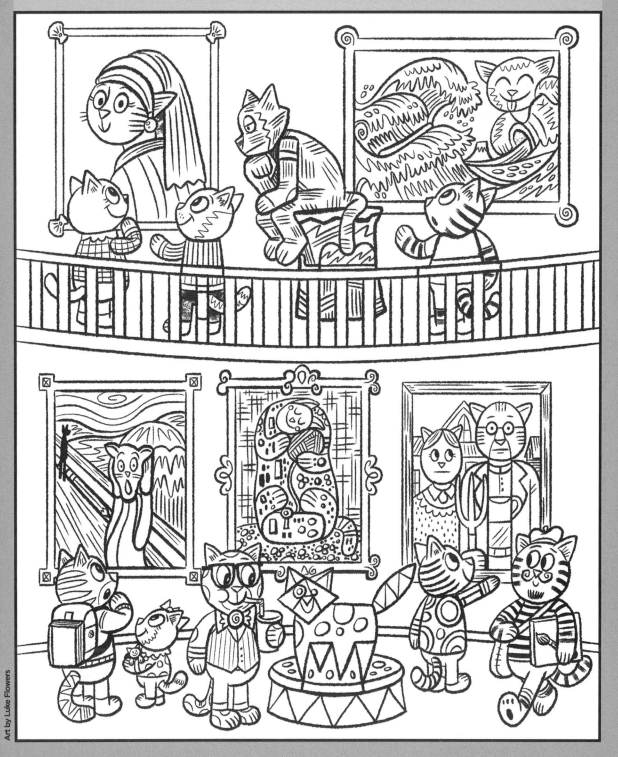

crown

umbrella

book

magnifying glass

pencil

paintbrush

slice of pizza

sunglasses

toothbrush

bone

hat

mug

candy

sock

Kitty's Fish Tank

bell

pencil

slice of bread

worm

carrot

ruler

lollipop

cookie

heart

crown

flag

golf club

mitten

fried egg

envelope

10

Art by Jannie Ho

Puppy Pilots

Sweet Dreams

artist's brush

bread

carrot

feather

heart

wishbone

wishbone

mushroom

bean

snail

candy cane

coffee mug

A Game of Chase

Family Road Trip

Taco Cats and *Purr*-itos

bowling ball

kite

crescent moon

ruler

spoon

paintbrush

crown

sunglasses

sailboat

ice skate

umbrella

heart

wrench

button

mushroom

On the Trail

lightning bolt

caterpillar

slice of pie

adhesive bandage

envelope

iron

paintbrush

snake

flag

ax

ruler

baseball mitt

butter knife

sailboat

banana

Art by Tamara Petrosino

Dr. Katz's Time Machine

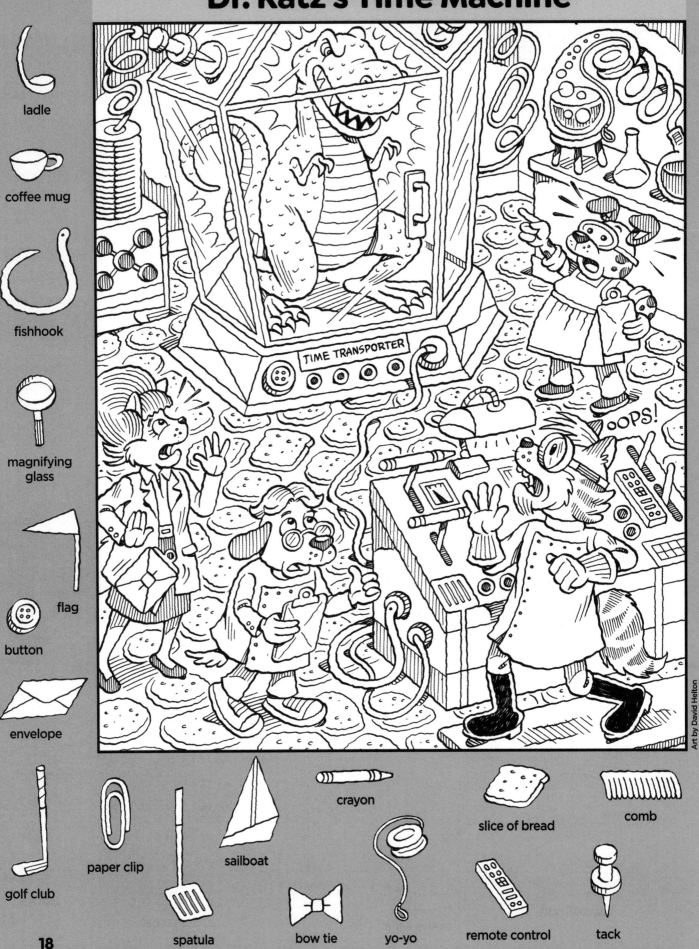

Cool Explorers

ice-cream cone

spoon

battery

banana

pickle

sock

flower

toothbrush

hairbrush

shoe

ruler

sneaker

comb

pencil

saw

eyeglasses

slice of pizza

rabbit

baseball bat

boomerang

saucepan

carrot

cheeseburger

candle

key

19

Pets in the Park

banana

baseball bat

bean

pencil

button

cane

 spoon

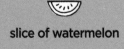 slice of watermelon

 donut

 dice

 fish

fork

 ring

spring

20

Kitty Slurps

ring

banana

comb

wedge of lemon

spoon

button

fish

slice of pizza

magnet

mushroom

flag

ruler

shoe

hat

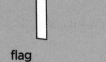
crown

crescent moon

Cool Cats

Burying His Bone

crown

ice-cream cone

pencil

T-shirt

banana

eyeglasses

heart

bell, squirrel, paper clip, spoon, glove, mushroom, bird, feather, fish, ring

25

Cozy Cuddlers

bell

teacup

envelope

crescent moon

candle

feather

golf club

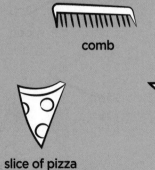
slice of pizza

comb

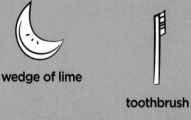
flag

wedge of lime

worm

toothbrush

heart

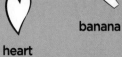
banana

Art by Tamara Petrosino

Pupp-eroni Pizzas

 birdie

 butterfly

 button

 clock

 flashlight

 fork

 paper clip

 fried egg

 sock

 present

 guitar

 hat

 key

mitten

canoe

Pet Wash

wedge of lemon

pencil

fish

scarf

tack

ruler

letter *E*

cinnamon bun

bell

crescent moon

slice of pizza

magnet

belt

sock

paper clip

seashell

domino

candle

button

snowman

envelope

fan

adhesive bandage

heart

29

Biking Buddies

slice of pizza

chili pepper

heart

hockey stick

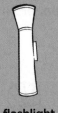
flashlight

artist's brush

carrot

toothbrush

lollipop

closed umbrella

pencil

mushroom

gem

worm

bowl

mitten

drinking cup

whistle

30

The Claw Salon

artist's brush

crown

glove

teacup

kite

open book

slice of bread

32

seashell

sock

teapot

worm

bird

banana

slice of pie

The Longest Doggy

fried egg

fishhook

horseshoe

lock

golf club

waffle

heart

crown

olive

arrow

34

banana

baseball

candle

bowling ball

golf club

comb

ruler

porcupine

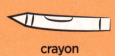
crayon

wedge of lime

Art by Tamara Petrosino

35

Which Dog Wins?

mitten

snake

fishhook

heart

snail

glove

domino

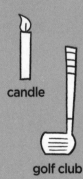
candle

golf club

crescent moon

funnel

needle

bell

measuring scoop

artist's brush

canoe

musical note

piece of popcorn

drumstick

paper airplane

butterfly

drinking straw

sailboat

ice-cream cone

36

Doggy's Bedtime

safety pin

cherry

shell

baseball

leaf

mitten

heart

balloon

ruler

button

fried egg

paper airplane

wedge of lemon

teacup

horseshoe

Art by Katie Wood

37

Lemonade, *Purr*-ty Please?

SUPER CHALLENGE Can you find 16 hidden pitchers in this scene?

Doggy's Trip to Space

flag

bell

bowl

candy cane

hockey stick

fish

sock

wedge of lemon

ring

ladle

sailboat

dinosaur

golf club

flashlight

slice of pizza

needle

fishhook

traffic light

39

Cat Community

crayon

crescent moon

slice of watermelon

seashell

slice of cake

vase

pine tree

slice of bread

worm

button

hamburger

Crafty Corgi-corns

Pet Picture Palooza

Cats in Boxes

ghost

bell

butterfly

shoe

pencil

umbrella

wedge of lime

ring

strawberry

mitten

ruler

key

olive

mouse

hat

Nap Time

needle

candle

pencil

bell

paper clip

 party horn

 heart

 ring

 bow tie

 light bulb

 sock

 wishbone

 toothbrush

 chili pepper

 broccoli

 tube of toothpaste

45

Kitty's Condo

Cat Summer Camp

spoon
artist's brush
toothbrush
bowling pin
banana
carrot
ladle
ice-cream cone
mitten
cupcake
book
kite
watering can
slice of pizza
sailboat
magnet
teacup
heart
ice-cream bar
scissors
traffic cone

Art by Jennifer Harney

Playground Pups

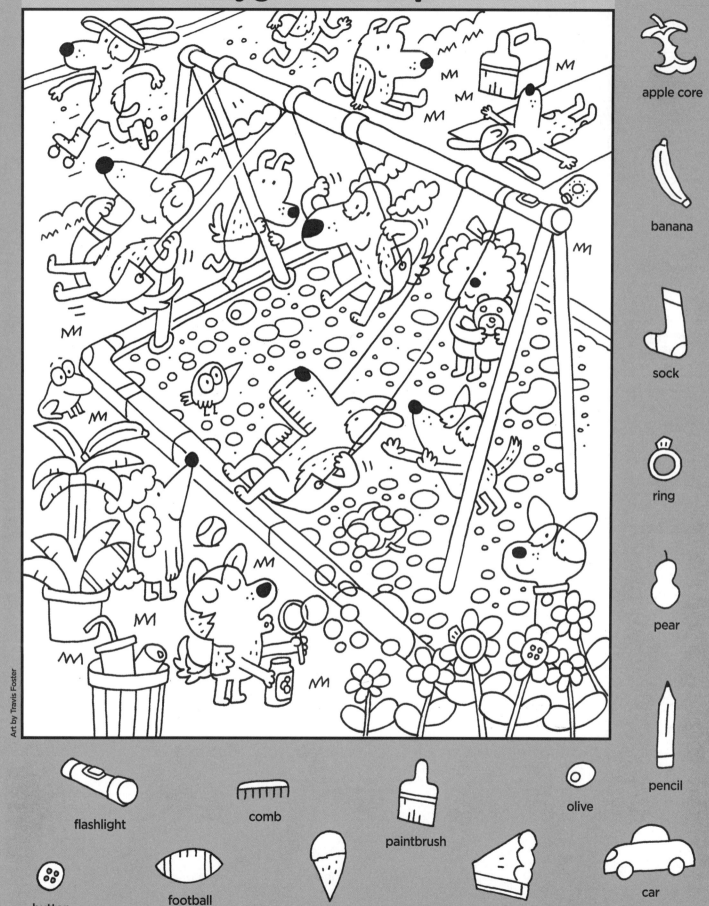

Underwater Pets

beehive

lollipop

candy

broccoli

cake

candy cane

 glove
 hat
 heart
 ice-cream bar
 bowl

Animal Construction Crew

Cat-erpillar's Forest

artist's brush

bacon

banana

tooth

spoon

fried egg

bell

ruler

glove

teacup

hat

fish

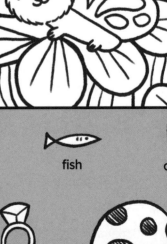
crown

heart

sailboat

fishhook

ring

ladybug

54

Puddle Jumpers

Summer Vacation

banana

candle

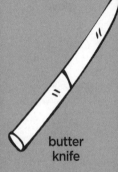
butter knife

ice-cream cone

worm

fork

mug

heart

sock

saw

crescent moon

56

megaphone

comb

ring

musical note

bowl

bell

pennant

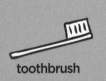
button

needle

nail

slice of cake

ladle

toothbrush

57

Making Biscuits

baseball bat

pan

golf club

pencil

shell

scissors

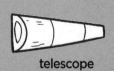
telescope

fish

eyeglasses

ruler

button

boomerang

crescent moon

sailboat

comb

magnifying glass

58

Kitty Cat Club

artist's brush

banana

candle

heart

funnel

coin

glove

caterpillar

toothpaste

canoe

Meow-ter Space

baseball bat

hat

pencil

ice-cream cone

toothbrush

slice of pizza

adhesive bandage

candy

sock

teacup

fried egg

football

cherry

shoe

car

Art by Luke Flowers

Walking the Dogs

bowl

pine tree

candle

clothespin

flag

ice-cream cone

crayon

pen

spoon

magnifying glass

Art by Ron Lieser

ruler

fish

heart

dolphin

glove

clock

horn

needle

pencil

snake

pear

slice of pie

zipper

bell

61

Dog Day at the Park

Feline Fruits

ax

bell

bow tie

horseshoe

hockey stick

sailboat

slice of pizza

paper airplane

ruler

candle

worm

crescent moon

envelope

toothbrush

heart

artist's brush

macaroni

test tube

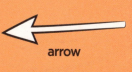
crown

arrow

65

Furry Foods

Backpack Buddies

Doggy Dash

banana

musical note

flag

flag

baseball bat

slice of pizza

cotton candy

comb

hammer

paper clip

ruler

needle

rainbow

ring

lollipop

wishbone

Art by Merrill Rainey

68

Sunken Treasure

artist's brush

comb

trowel

cupcake

iron

envelope

cake

fried egg

Shipshape

clock

ruler

baseball

envelope

slice of pie

domino

die

waffle

slice of watermelon

cracker

candy corn

button

Best in Show

oven mitt

ladle

crescent moon

funnel

candy

sailboat

flag

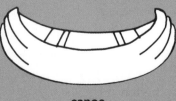
canoe

caterpillar

snake

slice of pie

snail

mushroom

banana

ice-cream bar

Park Romp

heart

horseshoe

bell

belt

crescent moon

ghost

seashell

hockey stick

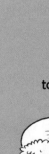
winter hat

toothbrush

ice-cream bar

ice-cream cone

broccoli

pencil

glove

carrot

slice of bread

cupcake

Scaredy-Dog

Fairy Friends

bell

banana

candle

comb

beach ball

umbrella

eggplant

present

saltshaker

crown

feather

needle

seed

necktie

crescent moon

fishhook

thimble

heart

 envelope

 fried egg

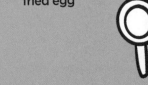 teacup

 magnifying glass

 ghost

 button

 sand dollar

77

Bone Appétit

artist's brush

butterfly

top hat

worm

canoe

ghost

kite

78

Lots of Stuffies

bacon

carrot

mug

heart

boomerang

olive
ladle

leaf

mushroom

beehive

lightning

flashlight

toothbrush

boot

duck

caterpillar

Art by Kyle Beckett

80

It's Bath Time!

toothbrush

ring

envelope

pacifier

heart

lollipop

golf club

baseball bat

ruler

canoe

light bulb

shoe

pencil

banana

slice of lemon

magnet

glove

ice-cream cone

baseball

paper clip

slice of pizza

82

Art by Dusty Hiestand

Lab-racadabra

Granny Dogs

baseball

banana

duck

ice-cream cone

flag

loaf of bread

bowling ball

wishbone

boomerang

thimble

toothbrush

84

lollipop

wedge of lemon

carrot

sailboat

golf club

crescent moon

sun

wedge of cheese

glove

cake

needle

85

Kittens in Mittens

bird

basketball

candle

tree

carrot

flashlight

slice of pizza

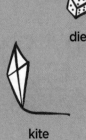
die

kite

watch

ice-cream cone

grapes

leaf

light bulb

turnip

shell

Get a Good Sniff

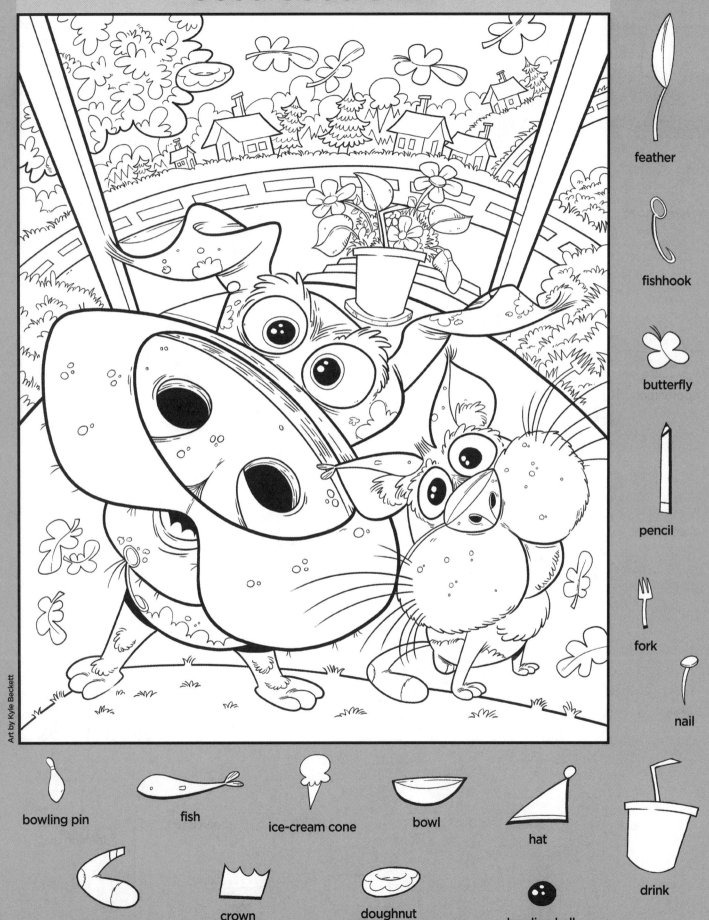

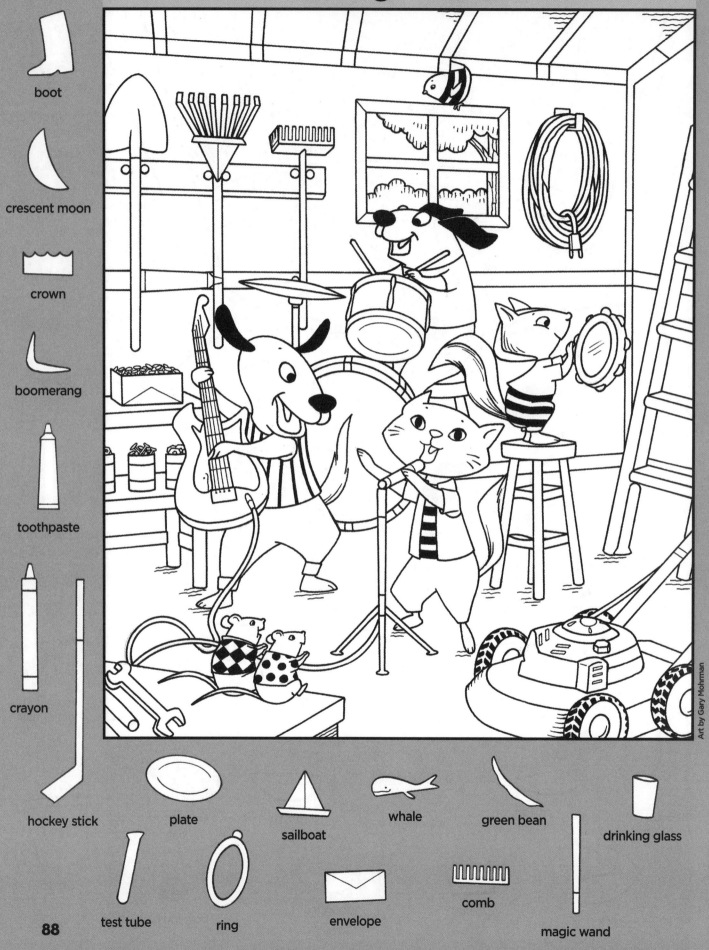

So Much Yarn!

magnifying glass

boomerang

light bulb

crescent moon

ice-cream cone

slice of pizza

necktie · book · hanger · sailboat · olive · lemon · ladder · microphone · letter T · ring · leaf · letter Y

Beagle Bagels

candle

crescent moon

sailboat

paper clip

mitten

feather

golf club

pennant

ruler

wishbone

ring

envelope

bell

heart

horseshoe

battery

Doggy's New Do

carrot

shoe

shopping cart

slice of pizza

fortune cookie

paper airplane

porcupine

ice-cream cone

spaceship

candle

cactus

chest

xylophone

mitten

peanut

Look Who's Home!

ice-cream bar

spatula

toothpaste

belt

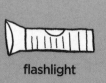
flashlight

pan

magnifying glass

pennant

baseball bat

bell

diamond

gavel

92

glove

hockey stick

kite

chef's hat

pencil

wedge of lemon

slice of pie

yo-yo

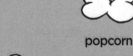
popcorn

spoon

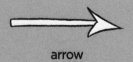
arrow

shell

Bulldog Meets Bullfrog

Cuddle Buddies

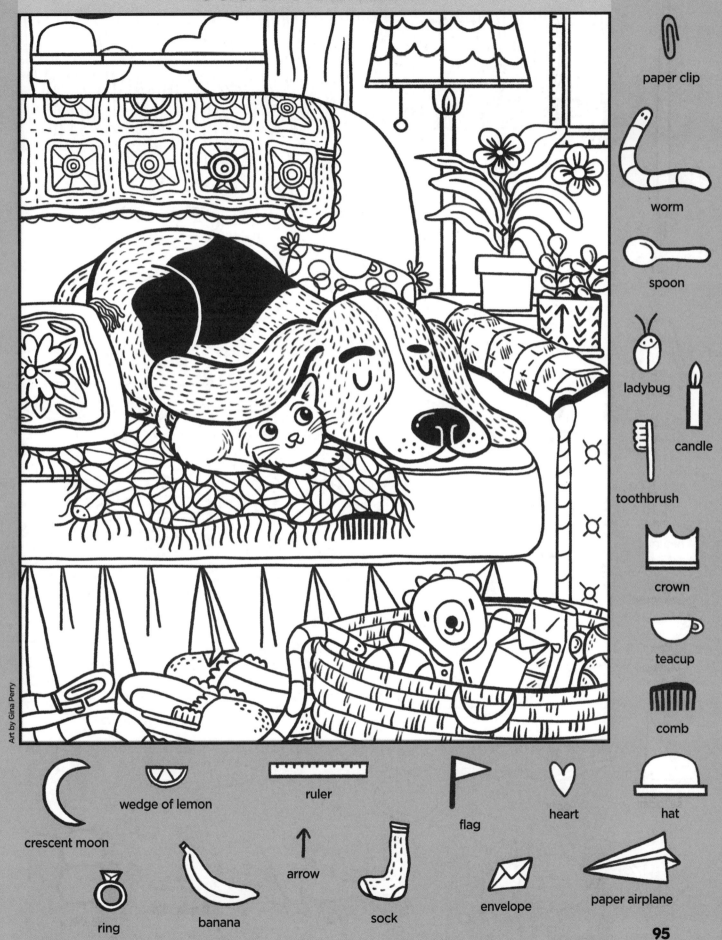

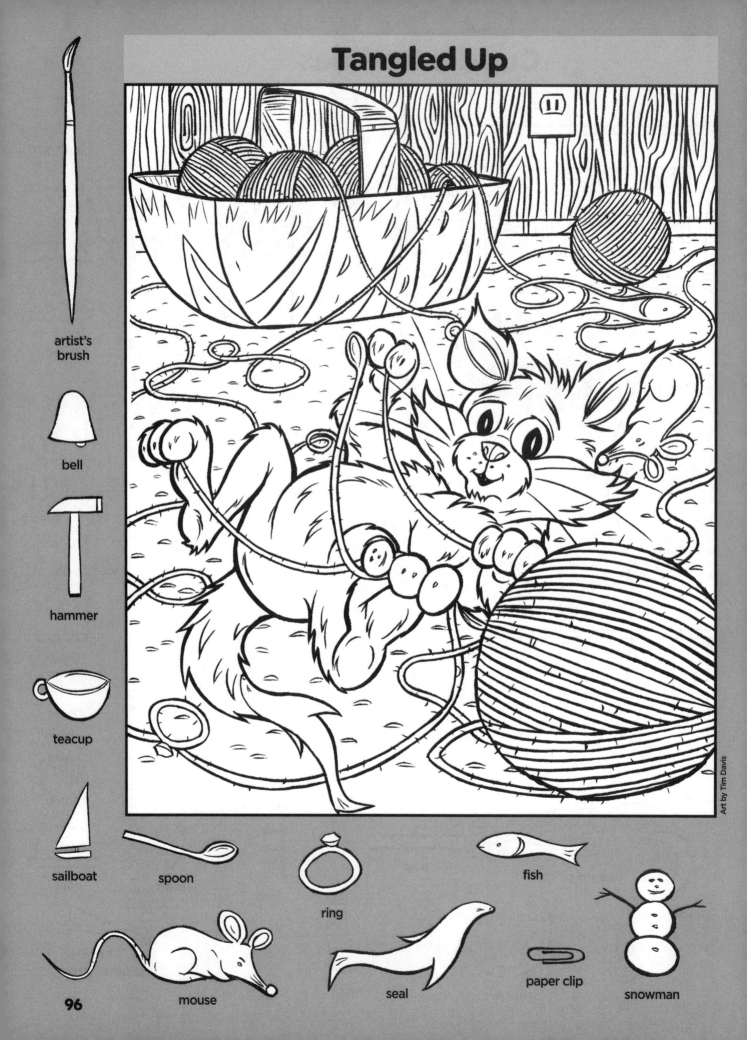

A New Friend

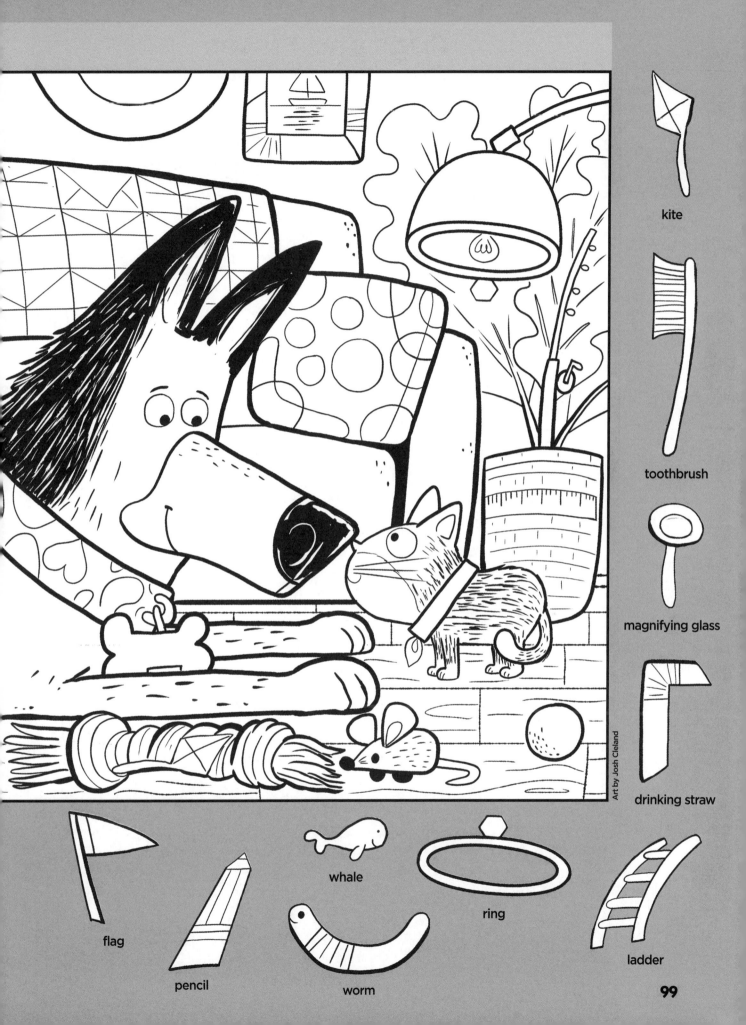

Pugs and Kisses

lamp

bowl

chili pepper

necktie

hanger

ladder

mushroom

saw

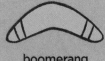
boomerang

pencil

slice of pizza

snake

mug

bacon

yo-yo

crown

Pups in Pajamas

Kit-teas

- baseball
- mushroom
- glove
- doughnut
- shoe
- carrot
- wedge of lemon
- drumstick
- yo-yo
- lightning
- spoon
- chili pepper
- lemon
- leaf
- tack
- heart
- crescent moon
- pencil

Dog Volleyball

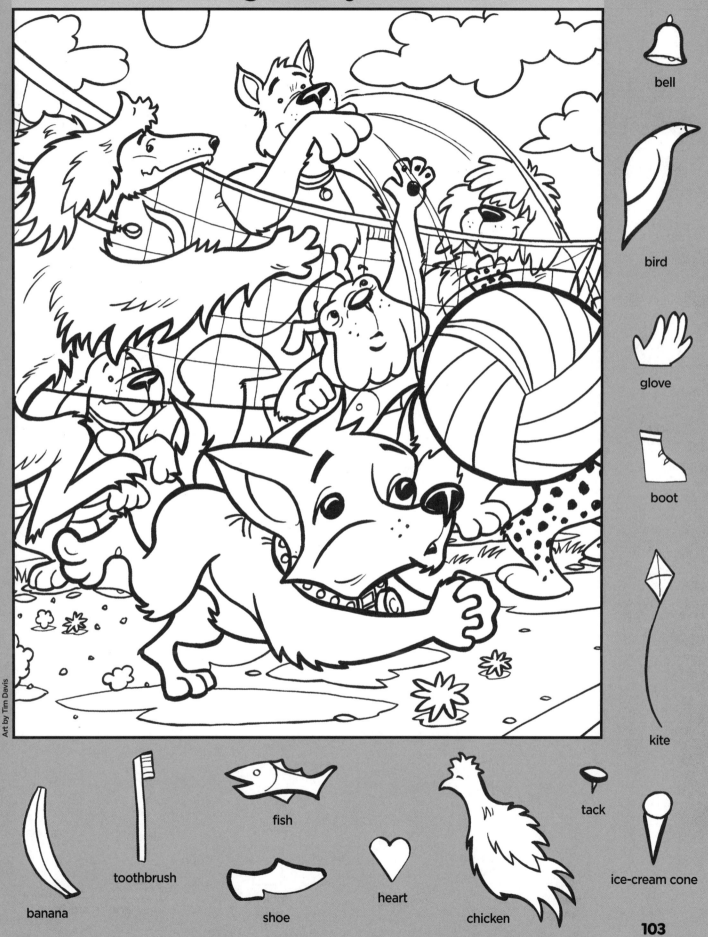

Poodles 'n' Noodles

brush

worm

heart

slice of pie

wishbone

ring

yarn

shoe

banana

wedge of lemon

umbrella

fishhook

window

pencil

105

The Coolest Cat Walk

banana

orange

paper airplane

compass

arrow

dice

puzzle piece

crescent moon

shell

hamburger

snake

106

leaf

lemon

kite

paper clip

horseshoe

wedge of lemon

flyswatter

cupcake

shell

slice of pizza

107

Kitten Cuddles

anchor

bell

carrot

sailboat

bird

comb

teacup

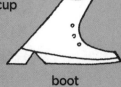
boot

fish

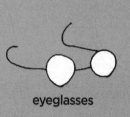
umbrella

eyeglasses

pencil

108

Raining Cats and Dogs

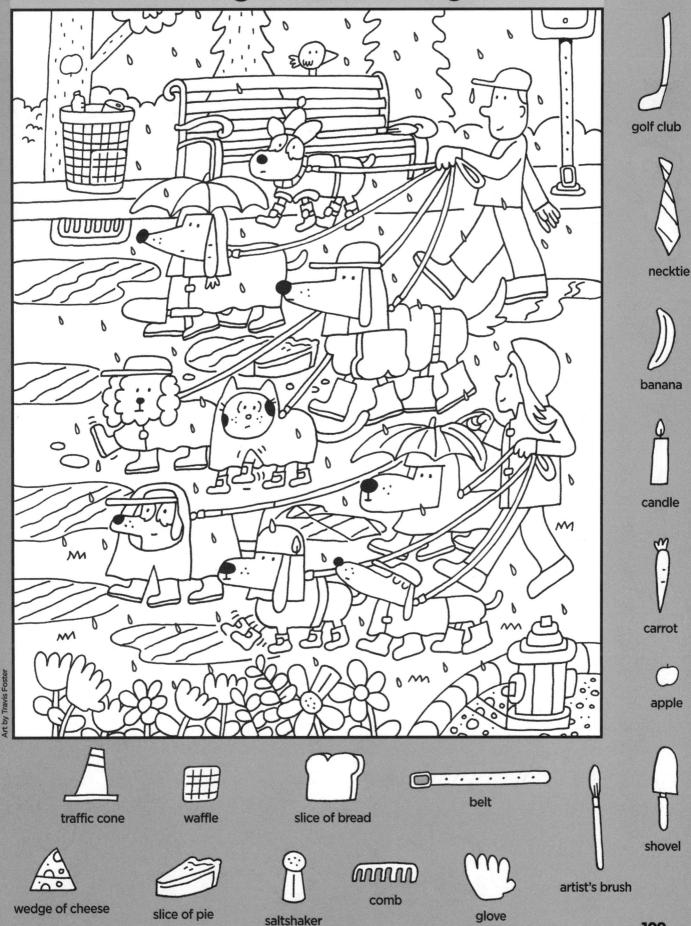

Dogsled

ring

saw

bell

pencil

comb

banana

ice-cream cone

open book

hat

fish

spoon

duck

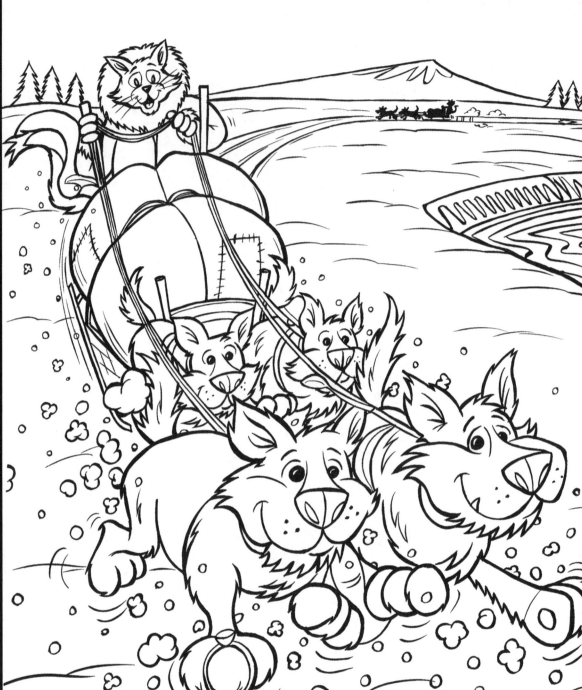

110

Apartment Kitty

A Cat Nap

toothbrush

golf club

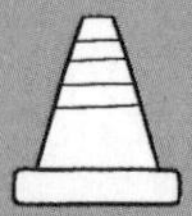

cone

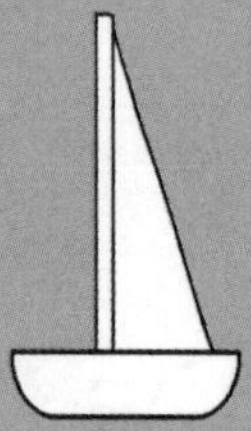

sailboat

ladder

ghost

eyeglasses

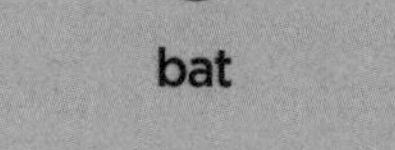

bat

shoe

fish

112

Animal Swap

boomerang

toothbrush

banana

briefcase

flower

crescent moon

slice of pizza

roller skate

ice-cream cone

glove

envelope

tennis racket

eyeglasses

button

lightning

Puppy Playtime

crescent moon

heart

ice-cream cone

umbrella

caterpillar

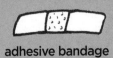
adhesive bandage

mushroom

worm

115

Ain't Nothin' but a Hound Dog

heart
comb
fishhook
hockey stick
snake
snail

pencil

crescent moon

envelope

boomerang

brush

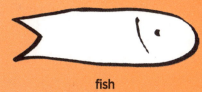
fish

Grand-dogs Calling

magnifying glass

whistle

bird

musical note

nail

candle

ladder

magnet

carrot

pencil

ladle

toothbrush

pizza

popcorn

watermelon

Art by Kyle Beckett

118

Dog Show

banana

book

heart

feather

bowl

pencil

shoe

ice pop

wishbone

nail

hammer

hat

119

Doggy Dance-Off!

sailboat

slice of pie

popcorn

tack

doughnut

traffic light

crayon

envelope

wedge of lemon

canoe

spoon

toothbrush

120

book

golf club

fried egg

button

flag

ruler

boomerang

drinking straw

cake

hammer

hamburger

121

Animal Zumba

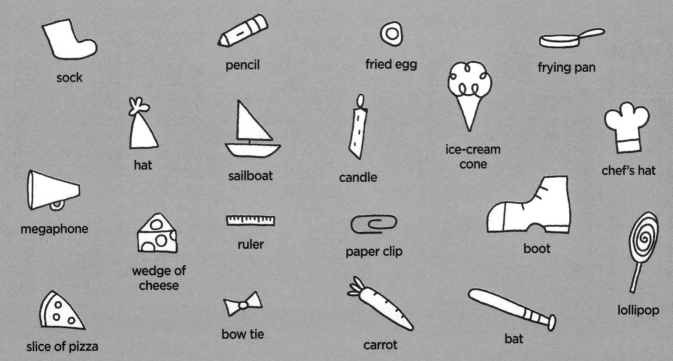

123

Feline Fairy Tale

bell

ice pops

heart

comb

carrot

candle

dog bone

slice of pizza

pear

lollipop

hot dog

horseshoe

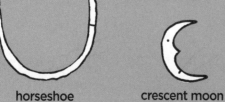
snake

ice-cream cone

crescent moon

caterpillar

toothbrush

snowman

muffin

mitten

124

Fluffy Cones

Window Kitties

Hide-and-Seek

magic wand

jar

hockey stick

crown

needle

leaf

cup

car

Super Dogs

flashlight

button

wedge of cheese

slice of pie

banana

ball

musical note

crown

ladder

ruler

heart

pen

wedge of lemon

hat

carrot

mug

artist's brush

boomerang

candy cane

pencil

Art by Merrill Rainey

Game Night

key

candle

thumbtack

adhesive bandage

envelope

crown

heart

toothbrush

 magnifying glass

 mitten

 button

 bone

 olive

 ring

 popcorn

Art by Shaw Nielsen

Answers

▼ Page 4

▼ Page 5

▼ Pages 6–7

▼ Page 8

▼ Page 9

▼ Page 10

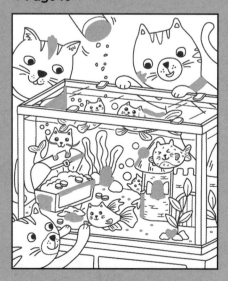

▼ Page 11

Answers

▼ **Pages 12–13**

▼ **Page 14**

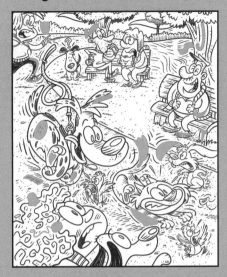

▼ **Page 15**

▼ **Page 16**

▼ **Page 17**

▼ **Page 18**

▼ **Page 19**

131

Answers

▼ Pages 20–21

▼ Page 22

▼ Page 23

▼ Page 24

▼ Page 25

▼ Page 26

▼ Page 27

132

Answers

▼ Pages 28–29

▼ Page 30

▼ Page 31

▼ Pages 32–33

▼ Pages 34–35

▼ Page 36

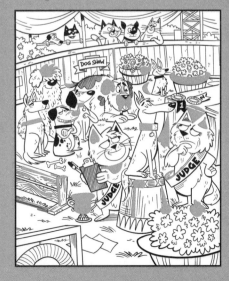

133

Answers

▼ Page 37

▼ Page 38

▼ Page 39

▼ Pages 40–41

▼ Page 42

▼ Page 43

▼ Page 44

▼ Page 45

Answers

▼ Page 46

▼ Page 47

▼ Page 48

▼ Page 49

▼ Pages 50–51

▼ Page 52

▼ Page 53

▼ Page 54

135

Answers

▼ Page 55

▼ Pages 56–57

▼ Page 58

▼ Page 59

▼ Page 60

▼ Page 61

▼ Page 62

▼ Page 63

Answers

▼ **Pages 64-65**

▼ **Page 66**

▼ **Page 67**

▼ **Page 68**

▼ **Page 69**

▼ **Pages 70-71**

▼ **Page 72**

137

Answers

▼ Page 73

▼ Page 74

▼ Page 75

▼ Pages 76-77

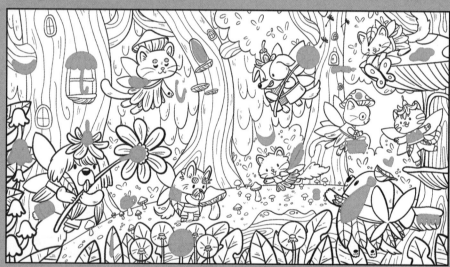

▼ Pages 78-79

▼ Page 80

138

Answers

▼ Page 81

▼ Page 82

▼ Page 83

▼ Pages 84–85

▼ Page 86

▼ Page 87
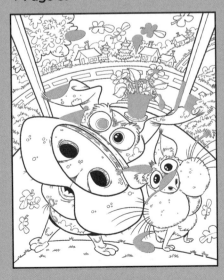

▼ Page 88

▼ Page 89

139

Answers

▼ Page 90

▼ Page 91

▼ Pages 92–93

▼ Page 94

▼ Page 95

▼ Page 96

▼ Page 97

Answers

▼ Pages 98–99

▼ Page 100

▼ Page 101

▼ Page 102

▼ Page 103

▼ Page 104

▼ Page 105

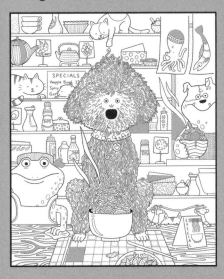

Answers

▼ **Pages 106–107**

▼ **Page 108**

▼ **Page 109**

▼ **Page 110**

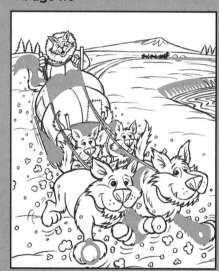

▼ **Page 111**

▼ **Pages 112–113**

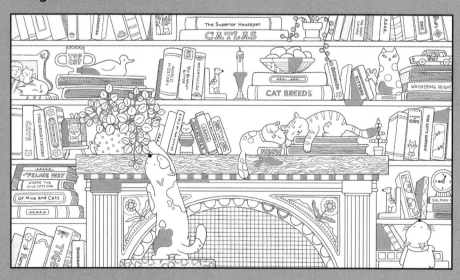

▼ **Page 114**

Answers

▼ Page 115

▼ Pages 116–117

▼ Page 118

▼ Page 119

▼ Pages 120–121

▼ Page 122

143

Answers

▼ Page 123

▼ Page 124

▼ Page 125

▼ Page 126

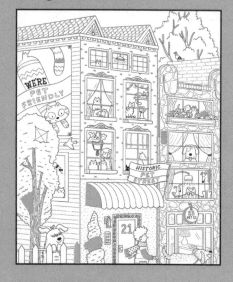

▼ Page 127

▼ Page 128

▼ Page 129

Copyright © 2025 by
Highlights for Children
All rights reserved.
Copying or digitizing this book for storage, display, or distribution in any other medium is strictly prohibited.

For information about permission to reproduce selections from this book, please contact permissions@highlights.com.

Published by Highlights Press
815 Church Street
Honesdale, Pennsylvania 18431
ISBN: 978-1-63962-292-4
Manufactured in Dongguan,
Guangdong, China
Mfg. 10/2024

First edition
Visit our website at Highlights.com.
10 9 8 7 6 5 4 3 2 1

144

It was the middle of the Great Depression and times were difficult. The ranch didn't have running water or electricity.

Yet Sandra's gap-toothed smile beamed. She loved life on the Lazy B Ranch.

In the 1930s, many people thought a girl's only job was to tidy the house and cook the meals. Boys were the ones who could herd cattle and fix fences. But that wasn't the case at the Lazy B.

Sandra galloped on horseback with cowboys through the rugged terrain. She painted screen doors and learned to change tires. She drove a truck as soon as she could see over the steering wheel.

There wasn't a school close to the ranch. Starting at six years old, Sandra spent the school year with her grandmother, who lived four hours away.

Each September Sandra took the train alone to El Paso, Texas. She watched as her parents and beloved ranch life disappeared into the distance.

Sandra did well in school. But she didn't feel like she belonged among the elegant surroundings of the Radford School for Girls. She missed the wide-open spaces of the Lazy B.

Then one year the school hosted a guest who made a lasting impression on Sandra.

First Lady Eleanor Roosevelt gave a speech to the students. Eleanor Roosevelt encouraged civic duty and became Sandra's first role model of a woman who served her country. Sandra's interest in public service would only grow.

When Sandra graduated from high school near the top of her class, many people thought girls shouldn't go to college.

Sandra had other ideas.

For two hot days, sixteen-year-old Sandra and her parents drove from Arizona across the desert to Stanford University in California.

As a young man, her father had dreamed of attending the same school, but his family needed him to work on the ranch instead. Now he was going to make sure Sandra didn't miss her chance.

The palm-tree-lined avenues and bright green lawns of Stanford were quite a contrast to the dusty roads and cacti of the Lazy B. And even though men far outnumbered women on campus, Sandra felt at home.

The more Sandra learned, the more she wanted to know.
She read about history and learned about democracy.

A professor spoke about the importance of serving the community.
He talked about how women should have the same rights as men.
Sandra agreed. She knew a woman could do anything a man could.

Many women married right after graduation, but Sandra had her own ideas about that, too. In the fall of 1950, she enrolled as one of only five women in Stanford University's law school.

Some people thought a woman shouldn't go to law school. Sandra disagreed. Her classmate John O'Connor did, too.

John respected Sandra's intelligence and he made her laugh. They spent day after day talking, studying, laughing. Soon they were inseparable.

Sandra worked hard and graduated near the top of her law school class. Like her classmates, she searched for a job with a law firm. But during the 1950s, law firms didn't want to hire a lawyer who was a woman. Only one firm would interview her. And they offered her a job as a secretary, not as a lawyer.

Sandra was shocked! She declined their offer. She was going to be a lawyer.

That winter Sandra and John were married at the Lazy B.

Then they returned to California. John joined a law firm while Sandra continued to search for a job as a lawyer.

Sandra heard the local government might have law jobs available to women.

So she contacted the district attorney. Sandra could work for him, but she wouldn't have an office, a desk, or a paycheck. She accepted the offer anyway. Finally, Sandra was researching cases and answering difficult legal questions.

Eventually, Sandra and John decided to move to Arizona and start a family. John returned to a law firm. But Sandra still couldn't find a single firm interested in hiring a lawyer who was a woman.

Sandra decided that if a law firm wouldn't hire her, she would open her own. She and another attorney rented space at a mall and started their own law office.

Over the years, as Sandra's family grew, she wanted to spend more time with them. She left her law practice to stay home with her three young sons.

But she still wanted to make a difference in the lives of others, too.

Sandra's belief in public service had blossomed since seeing Eleanor Roosevelt in grade school and learning about democracy in college.

So she volunteered in her community and became involved in local politics.

Sandra had worked hard her whole life. She was smart. Skilled. Self-reliant. Yet she still didn't have the same opportunities as men. Sandra knew that women across the United States faced the same prejudice she did. She also understood that the laws discriminating against women needed to change.

By 1969, Sandra was well known for her community service and admired for her leadership. When there was an opening in the Arizona State Senate, the governor asked her to fill it. She accepted the job.

When Sandra ran for reelection the following year, she won! Within three years, Sandra was elected the Senate majority leader.

She was the first woman in the country to hold this position.

Although women were allowed to work in the state senate, it had always been a man's territory. Many mocked Sandra. Several called her nasty names.

Sandra tried to ignore their insults, but being bullied is painful.

Sandra's heart pounded and her legs trembled when the men made fun of her. Once, she left the senate chamber and went to the bathroom to cry.

Maybe these men were right. Should she give up?

Certainly not. No one told Sandra what she could and couldn't do.

So she wiped away her tears and went to work.

Sandra gathered a list of all the laws in Arizona that treated women unfairly—400 laws! She worked to change each one.

Sandra continued to work hard in her next job, too.

In 1975, she became an Arizona state judge. Sandra listened to lawyers and ruled on cases.

She carefully considered every decision she made. Sandra knew her decisions would have a lasting impact on the everyday people in her courtroom.

Four years later, she rose to the Arizona Court of Appeals.

Judge O'Connor's reputation for fairness spread across the country, where a new opportunity awaited. A big one. The most important legal cases in the United States are decided by the nine justices of the Supreme Court in Washington, D.C. In 1981, one justice planned to retire.

There had never been a woman on the Supreme Court, the highest court in the country. Sandra doubted a ranch girl from Arizona could ever be nominated to be a Supreme Court justice.

Then the president of the United States and fellow Westerner, Ronald Reagan, asked to meet her.

Could Sandra really become the first woman Supreme Court justice in United States history? Could she decide the most difficult cases facing the nation? Could she sit along the mahogany bench where only men had served?

Yes. Yes, she could.

One week later, President Reagan nominated Sandra Day O'Connor to the Supreme Court.

On September 25, 1981, Sandra Day O'Connor took the constitutional oath and became the first woman to be a Supreme Court justice in United States history.

"I will well and faithfully discharge the duties of the office on which I am about to enter."

As Justice Sandra Day O'Connor walked down the steps of the Supreme Court building with that same gap-toothed smile, children around the country saw what was possible.

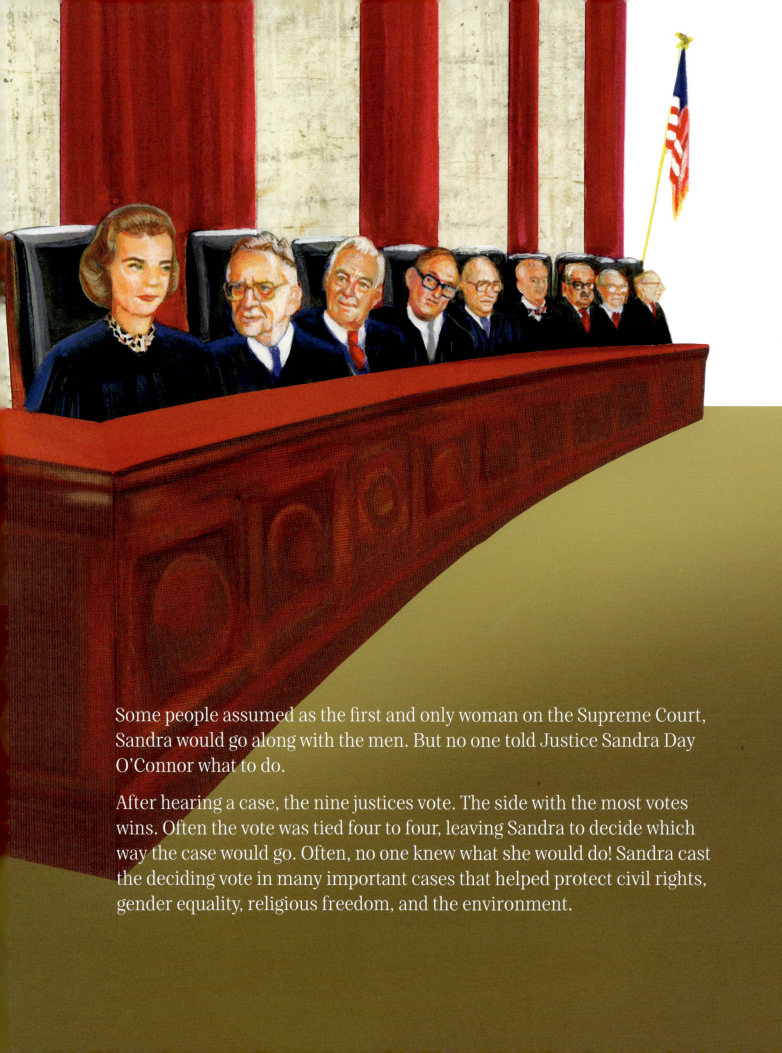

Some people assumed as the first and only woman on the Supreme Court, Sandra would go along with the men. But no one told Justice Sandra Day O'Connor what to do.

After hearing a case, the nine justices vote. The side with the most votes wins. Often the vote was tied four to four, leaving Sandra to decide which way the case would go. Often, no one knew what she would do! Sandra cast the deciding vote in many important cases that helped protect civil rights, gender equality, religious freedom, and the environment.

Sandra believed people could learn from each other when they came together. She insisted all the justices meet for lunch once a week. Sometimes she sat in their office until they agreed to join.

From 1981 to 2006, Sandra Day O'Connor served as a Supreme Court justice of the United States of America. Her legacy stretches from the Lazy B's western mountains to the Supreme Court's marble hallways. She opened doors for girls, women, and others who face discrimination to have more opportunity.

Sandra Day O'Connor will always be the first. But because of her work, she won't be the last.

"Sandra Day O'Connor is like the pilgrim in the poem she sometimes quotes who has forged a new trail and built a bridge behind her for all young women to follow."
—President Barack Obama
(when awarding Justice O'Connor the Presidential Medal of Freedom)

"Sandra was as close as I came to having a big sister."
—Justice Ruth Bader Ginsburg

"Sandra was a warm and caring colleague, always practical but also an unyielding visionary about the role of the Court in our society."
—Justice Sonia Sotomayor

"Justice O'Connor never stopped thinking and listening, learning and growing. She judged with wisdom. And her service left both this Court and this Nation better."
—Justice Elena Kagan

"Because of her sharp mind, she became a pivotal justice who has left her mark on American constitutional law. Because of her indomitable spirit, she made the job uniquely hers. Sandra Day O'Connor was the perfect trailblazer."
—Justice Amy Coney Barrett

"Justice O'Connor helped pave the road on which other jurists, including me, now walk. Her story has inspired generations of lawyers and generations of Americans, and her commitment to justice and to the rule of law continues to serve as a model to us all."
—Judge Ketanji Brown Jackson

Sandra Day O'Connor's appointment to the Supreme Court opened many doors for women in the legal profession. Today, four out of the nine Supreme Court justices are women.

The work Sandra accomplished throughout her career also advanced women's rights. Before Sandra joined the Arizona State Senate, Arizona had laws that limited women, such as controlling what a woman could and couldn't buy without her husband's permission. By the time she left, she had helped change more than 400 of them. As a Supreme Court justice, she was the deciding vote in more than 300 cases, including decisions that protected civil rights, privacy, and protection against discrimination.

Throughout her life, Sandra encouraged citizens to be active participants in the government and inspired others to do what she called "work worth doing." In a letter to her sons, Sandra wrote of the importance of helping others. She believed it was a person's purpose, including her own.

After Sandra retired from the Supreme Court, she started the iCivics program, a free online civics program for middle-school students. She also continued to advocate around the world for what she believed in: democracy, equal justice under the law, and the rule of law. She even carried a copy of the Constitution in her pocketbook.

Sandra Day O'Connor died on December 1, 2023. She is remembered for her intelligence, wit, fairness, decency, grit, and grace.

"Each of us brings to our job, whatever it is, our lifetime of experiences and values."
—Justice Sandra Day O'Connor

Sandra Day O'Connor being sworn in, U.S. Supreme Court

KEY TERMS

Government
A government is a system in which a group of people use laws and leaders to maintain order, provide services, and defend land. The different levels of government in the United States are **city**, **state**, and **federal** (country).

Democracy
A form of government in which citizens vote to have a say in how the government is run.

Constitution
A constitution is a written plan that explains how a government works. A constitution establishes what the branches of the government are and what powers they have. It also lays out the rights of the citizens and the laws they must follow. A constitution may be added to or changed through a complex process. The Constitution of the United States took effect in 1789.

Lawyer
A lawyer is a person who represents clients in legal matters or in a court of law. Lawyers go to school after college and must pass a special test to represent others.

Branches of Government
There are three branches in the United States government. The president is the head of the **executive branch**. The vice president and the president's advisors are also part of this branch. The president signs and enforces laws, negotiates treaties, appoints judges, and issues orders.

The **legislative branch** is made up of the **House of Representatives** and the **Senate**—together they are called **Congress**. Congress writes laws for the president to sign, can declare war, and can **impeach** (formally accuse) a government official of a crime and remove them from office. Each state also has its own legislative branch—to create local laws. Sandra Day O'Connor worked in the state legislature branch in Arizona.

The **judicial branch** is made up of the country's court system. It interprets the Constitution and settles disagreements about the meanings of the laws.

Checks and Balances
A system in which each branch of government has different but equal responsibilities. It makes sure no one branch has too much authority.

The Supreme Court
The United States Supreme Court is the highest court in the **judicial branch**. The Supreme Court currently has nine members, called **justices**. A justice is nominated by the president and voted on by the Senate. A Supreme Court justice interprets the Constitution and applies their interpretations to legal cases. The justices vote, and the side with the most votes wins the case. A person is a Supreme Court justice for the rest of their life or until they decide to retire.

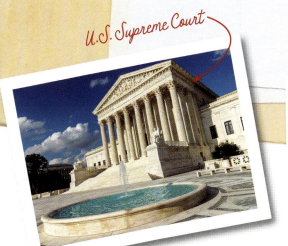
U.S. Supreme Court

U.S. Constitution

To Dave

—*Molly*

For the girls and women in my life who do it all with grit and determination, despite the ongoing barriers

—*Julia*

Text Copyright © 2025 Molly Golden
Illustration Copyright © 2025 Julia Breckenreid
Design Copyright © 2025 Sleeping Bear Press

Publisher expressly prohibits the use of this work in connection with the development of any software program, including, without limitation, training a machine learning or generative artificial intelligence (AI) system.

All rights reserved.
No part of this book may be reproduced in any manner without the express written consent of the publisher, except in the case of brief excerpts in critical reviews and articles. All inquiries should be addressed to:

SLEEPING BEAR PRESS™

2395 South Huron Parkway, Suite 200, Ann Arbor, MI 48104
www.sleepingbearpress.com © Sleeping Bear Press

Printed and bound in the United States
10 9 8 7 6 5 4 3 2 1

Library of Congress Cataloging-in-Publication Data
Names: Golden, Molly, author. | Breckenreid, Julia, illustrator.
Title: No one told Sandra Day O'Connor what to do : the first woman to serve on the United States Supreme Court / Molly Golden, Julia Breckenreid.
Description: Ann Arbor : Sleeping Bear Press, 2025. | Audience: Ages 6-10 | Summary: "The life of Sandra Day O'Connor is chronicled, from her early Arizona childhood, up through the many obstacles she faced in her professional career, before becoming the first woman to serve as a United States Supreme Court Justice"– Provided by publisher.
Identifiers: LCCN 2024034954 | ISBN 9781534113268 (hardcover)
Subjects: LCSH: O'Connor, Sandra Day, 1930-2023–Juvenile literature. | Judges–United States–Biography–Juvenile literature. | United States. Supreme Court–Officials and employees–Biography–Juvenile literature.
Classification: LCC KF8745.O25 G65 2025 | DDC 347.73/2634 [B]–dc23/eng/20240731 | LC record available at https://lccn.loc.gov/2024034954

Photos: Sandra Day O'Connor Being Sworn in a Supreme Court Justice by Chief Justice Warren Burger courtesy of Wikimedia Commons | U.S. Supreme Court: lucky-photographer / Alamy Stock Photo | U.S. Constitution: Mark Hayes / Alamy Stock Photo | Voting Booth: Andriy Popov / Alamy Stock Photo